C DYNAMITE EXPLODE

T CHAMPIONSHIP OF THE WORLD

XING

NIGHT

EVENT- 10 ROUNDS

EATEST OF ALL TIME !

To the Champion, Muhammad Ali. — J. H.

For my dad, Chu, who loves boxing. — E. V.

Text copyright © 2002 by Jim Haskins
Illustrations copyright © 2002 by Eric Velasquez

First published in the United States of America in 2002 by Walker Publishing Company, Inc.

Published simultaneously in Canada by Fitzhenry and Whiteside, Markham, Ontario L3R 4T8

For information about permission to reproduce selections from this book, write to Permissions, Walker & Company, 435 Hudson Street, New York, New York 10014

Library of Congress Cataloging-in-Publication Data

Haskins, James, 1941-
    Champion : the story of Muhammad Ali / Jim Haskins ; illustrations by Eric Velasquez.
      p. cm.
    Summary: A biography of Muhammad Ali, from his childhood in Louisville, Kentucky, his legendary boxing career, and his conversion to Islam, and opposition to the war in Vietnam, to his appearance at the 1996 summer Olympics in Atlanta.
      ISBN 0-8027-8784-3 — ISBN 0-8027-8785-1 (rein)
1. Ali, Muhammad, 1942—Juvenile literature. 2. Boxers (Sports)—United States—Biography—Juvenile literature.
[1. Ali, Muhammad, 1942- 2. Boxers (Sports) 3. African Americans—Biography.] I. Velasquez, Eric, ill. II. Title.

GV1132.A44.H36 2001
796.83'092—dc21
[B]
                                                       2001045374

The illustrations were painted in oil on Fabriano paper.

Book design by Marva J. Martin

Visit Walker & Company's Web site at www.walkerbooks.com

Printed in Hong Kong

10 9 8 7 6 5 4 3 2 1

CHAMPION: THE STORY OF MUHAMMAD ALI

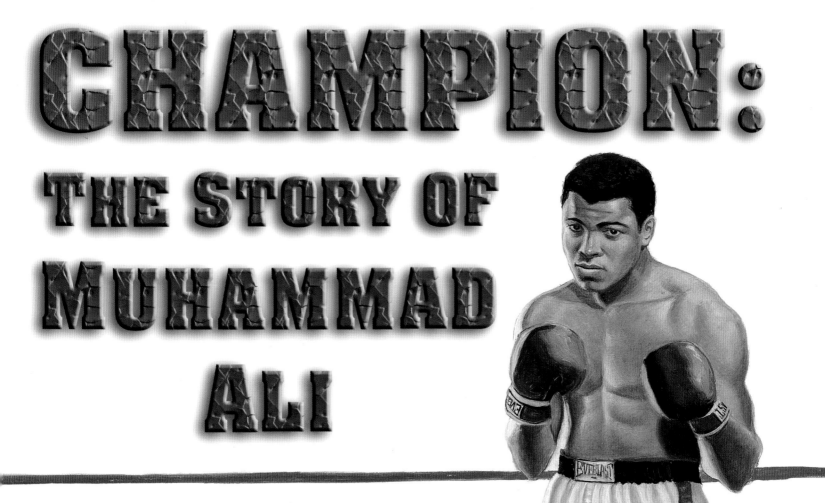

Jim Haskins

Illustrations by
Eric Velasquez

Walker & Company
New York

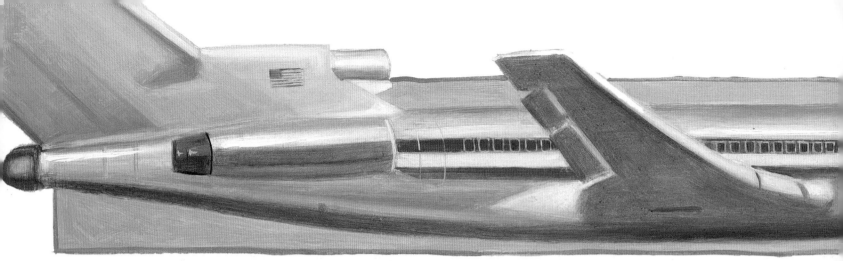

Muhammad Ali was riding in an airplane one time. Although he didn't like flying, he realized it gave him a special view of the world. He looked out the window and down to the earth below him. "I could hitchhike around the world," he thought. No matter where he was, someone would know him. Someone would feed him. Someone would give him a place to sleep. He was probably the most famous person alive.

He was the heavyweight boxing champion of the world. Some said he was the greatest boxer in history. Everyone said he was the fastest. He was more than that. He was a new kind of boxer. He lived a clean life and had never been in jail. He was deeply religious. He did not like to hurt anybody. He had helped change the image of professional boxing from a brutal pastime to a widely popular sport. He also had shown the world that he could be true to himself and his beliefs and still be a winner.

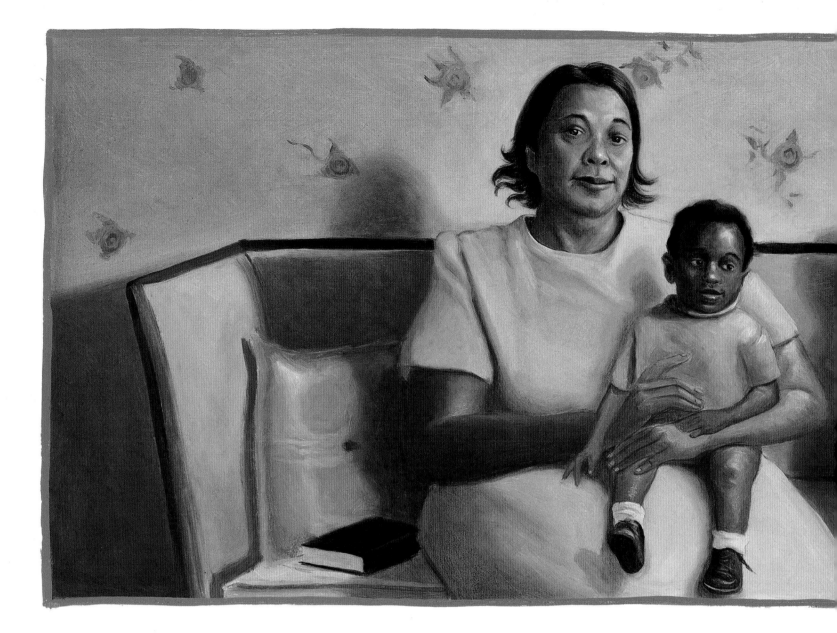

Muhammad Ali was born on January 17, 1942, in Louisville, Kentucky. He was named Cassius Marcellus Clay Jr. after his father. He was also named after a nineteenth-century white plantation owner who had freed all his slaves and worked to end slavery. Cassius Jr.'s great grandfather had grown up on that first Cassius Clay's land in Kentucky.

His father was a sign painter who loved to talk and make jokes. Cassius began to talk at a young age and also liked to make jokes. Not only did he tell jokes, he was a practical joker.

Cassius's mother, Odessa Clay, earned money for food by cooking and cleaning for white people. She was very religious. She read the Bible every day and took Cassius and his brother, Rudy, to church every Sunday.

Cassius grew up in a time when blacks were forced to stay apart from whites. He and Rudy had to go to a school for blacks. Like most other blacks in Louisville then, the Clays were quite poor. There was no school bus for black kids, and the Clays didn't have enough money to pay bus fare for both boys. So they usually had to walk to and from school. Young Cassius announced that he wanted to be rich one day, but his father told him he could never be rich because his skin was not white. Although he was basically a happy child, Cassius sometimes cried himself to sleep over what his people had to suffer.

For his twelfth birthday, Cassius received a shiny red bicycle. It was stolen almost as soon as he got it. Angry and upset, Cassius wanted to find the thief and beat him up. A policeman told Cassius that he had better learn how to fight first. Cassius never got his bike back. He got a mission in life instead.

    The policeman ran a gym. He offered to teach Cassius to box. Cassius decided that boxing as a sport was more important than fighting in anger. He learned that there were many famous black boxers. In fact, there were more black boxers in the United States than there were white boxers. Boxing was a way he could become rich and famous. He went to the gym every chance he got. He ate and drank only healthy things. He began running five miles every morning. He also started racing the bus to school.

Cassius got better and better at boxing. He was very fast. He had quick reflexes. While he was in junior high and high school, Cassius fought in amateur bouts. Talkative and funny, he started predicting in what round of the fight he would knock out his opponents. He made up silly poems to tell reporters when they interviewed him. One went like this:

This guy must be done
I'll stop him in one

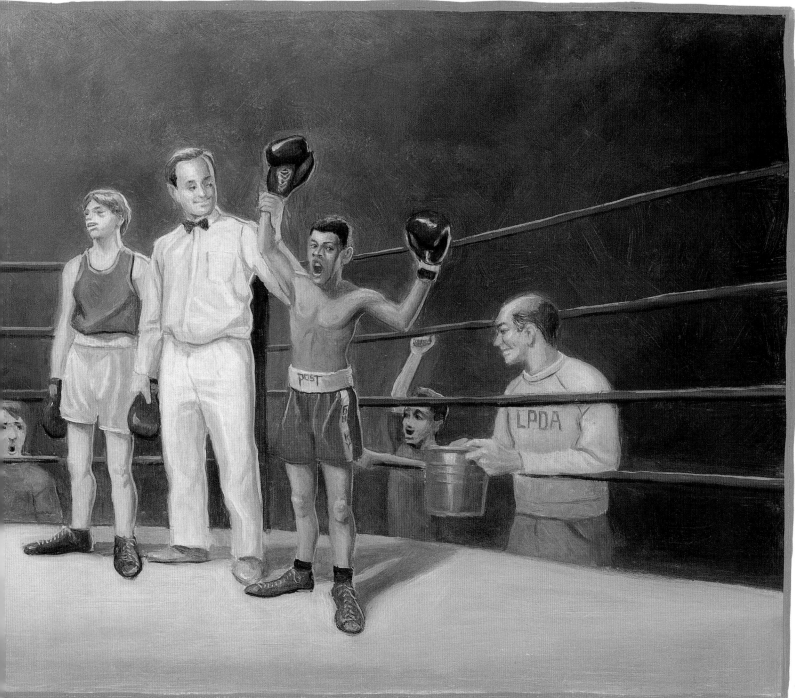

By the time he was eighteen, he had won one hundred amateur fights. These included four national boxing championships. He had lost only eight bouts.

In 1960, the Summer Olympics were held in Rome, Italy. Cassius tried out and made the U.S. Olympic boxing team as a light heavyweight. He was so afraid of flying that he bought his own parachute in an army surplus store and wore it on the flight to Rome.

In Rome, Cassius met Wilma Rudolph, a young black woman from Harlem in New York City. She was an inspiring athlete who had won three gold medals in running at the Olympic Games. Cassius had a crush on Rudolph, but she was already engaged to another runner.

Cassius fought four Olympic bouts. He beat fighters from Australia, Belgium, Poland, and Russia to win the Olympic gold medal. He was so proud of that medal that he wore it to bed at night.

Back at home, his father painted the front steps of the house red, white, and blue. The city of Louisville gave Cassius a hero's welcome. Cassius recited a special poem for the occasion, making reference to a figure in Roman history who was also named Cassius. It began:

To make America the greatest is my goal
So I beat the Russian and I beat the Pole
And for the U.S.A. won the Medal of Gold
Italians said, "You're greater than
the Cassius of Old" . . .

Not long afterward, Cassius Clay walked into a restaurant and ordered a glass of orange juice. The owner would not serve him because he was black. Cassius was angry and hurt. He says that the pain he felt was like having to take punches without hitting back.

After the Olympics, Cassius turned professional. From then on, he fought for money. A group of local white businessmen paid his expenses. They hired a white boxing trainer named Angelo Dundee.

At six feet three inches tall and weighing almost two hundred pounds, Cassius was now a heavyweight boxer. He had the same quickness as when he was twelve. He also had the same loud mouth. People called him "The Louisville Lip" and "Blabber Mouth." He didn't care.

He bragged:

**They all must fall
In the round I call**

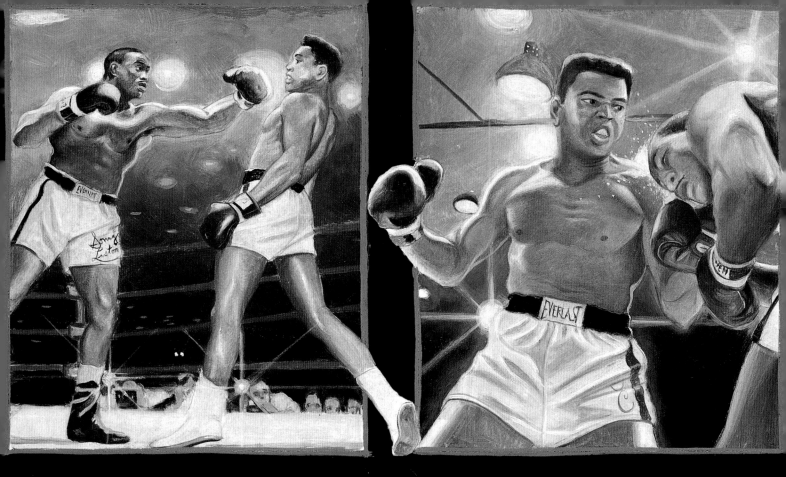

In 1964, Cassius went up against the heavyweight champion of the world. Sonny Liston was an ex-convict, backed by the mafia. Cassius boasted:

Sonny Liston is great
But he'll fall in eight

Secretly, he was scared. Liston was older and bigger and a brutal fighter. Cassius knew he could get hurt. Sports reporters were predicting that he would be knocked out in the first round.

Cassius knew the only way he could beat Liston was to be smarter than him. One of his trainers said he would have to "Float like a butterfly, sting like a bee." That was the way Cassius fought Liston. He danced around the bigger man. He dodged Liston's fists round after round. When he saw that Liston was getting tired, he started throwing punches. Many of them found their target. Liston refused to come out of his corner for round seven.

Cassius Clay was heavyweight champion of the world. Raising his arms in victory, he shouted,

"I am the king! I am the king!"

Then he looked down at the reporters who had predicted he would lose. He shook his fist at them and cried,

"Eat your words! Eat your words!"

The day after he beat Sonny Liston, Cassius Clay made a surprising announcement. He was no longer a Christian. He was now a member of the Nation of Islam, also known as the Black Muslims. The Nation was a militant black organization that not only taught blacks to be proud of themselves but also preached that they should keep themselves separate from whites. It claimed to follow the beliefs of the world religion of Islam, although Islam does not preach racial separation. Followers of Islam, who are called Muslims, worship God and call him Allah. Cassius had been interested in the Black Muslims since high school. He admired Elijah Muhammad, their leader, and Malcolm X, the minister whose fiery speeches had attracted many new members to the Nation. Black Muslims often took new names to honor their Muslim faith, or as a sign that they rejected their place in white American society. Some, like Malcolm X, used an X for their last name. Cassius Clay took a whole new Islamic name: Muhammad Ali.

Like Muslims all over the world, Muhammad Ali prayed to Allah five times a day. He also prayed in the boxing ring before every bout. He attended Nation of Islam temples and world Muslim mosques wherever he could find them. He married a Muslim woman. He did not have to change his habits of eating a healthy diet and being clean; he had always lived that way—especially since he had started boxing. Officials of the Nation took over management of his boxing career, but Ali kept his white trainer, Angelo Dundee.

Over the next two years, Muhammad Ali defended his world title several times, fighting British, German, Canadian, and American opponents, including a rematch with Sonny Liston. He was at the top of his form, and he kept the world heavyweight title for a total of three years. There is no telling how long he would have remained champion.

In 1967, the United States was deeply involved in the Vietnam War. U.S. troops were helping South Vietnam fight against the Vietcong of North Vietnam. Young men across the country were being called to serve in the army. Muhammad Ali refused to join the army, saying,

Keep asking me, no matter how long
On the war in Viet Nam, I sing this song
"I ain't got no quarrel with them Vietcong."

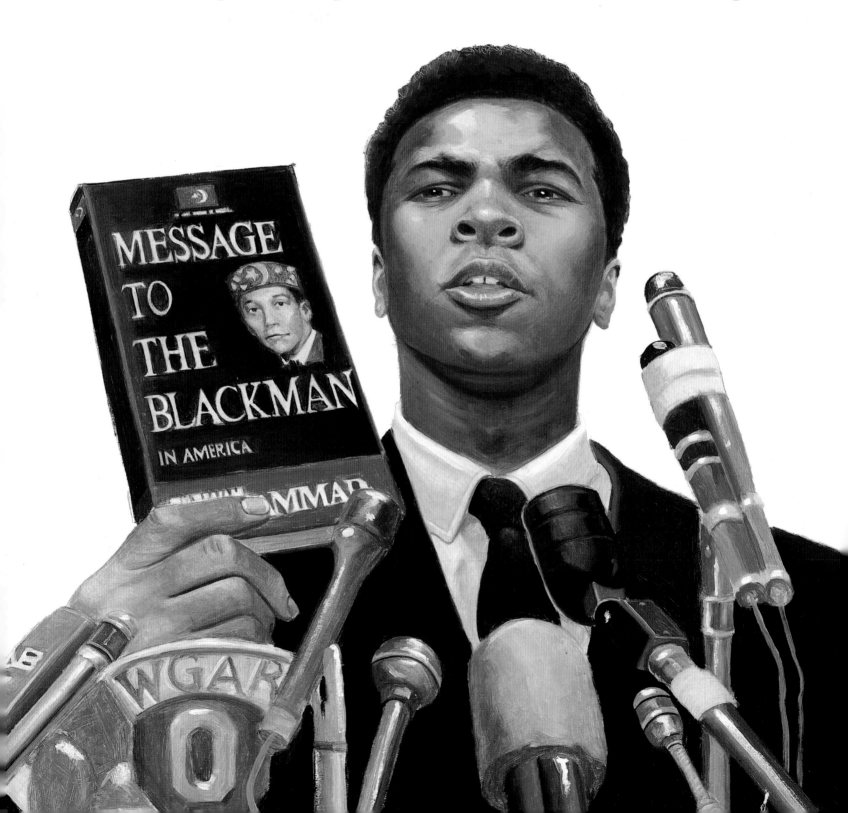

The United States had outlawed racial segregation while Ali was heavyweight champion of the world. Nevertheless, blacks were still denied many opportunities. It would be a long time before they enjoyed equality with whites. Ali said he did not believe in fighting for freedom for other people when his own people were not free. Members of the Nation of Islam did not serve in the military. In those days, they did not get involved in politics or even vote. Muhammad Ali said it was against his religion to join the army.

The United States government charged him with the crime of refusing military service and prosecuted him for draft evasion. Ali was sentenced to pay a fine and spend five years in jail. He was allowed to remain free while he appealed the verdict to a higher court, but he was banned from boxing and his title was taken away from him. Most people believed he was guilty.

The ban was a terrible blow to Muhammad Ali's career. He did not have a professional boxing match for nearly four years. As other heavyweight boxers won and lost the championship, Ali insisted that the title was still his. Until someone beat him in the ring, he believed that he remained the true champion.

Ali spent his years of exile speaking out against the Vietnam War. During this difficult time, he drew strength from his faith. Islam had helped him overcome other challenges in the past. It helped him conquer his fear of flying, and had enabled him to take his first trip to Africa, where there are many Muslims. Ali learned that unlike the Nation of Islam, world Islam is not antiwhite. All true believers are accepted. As had Malcolm X before him, he would one day break away from the radical Nation of Islam and devote himself to world Islam.

Eventually the Supreme Court, the highest court in the land, recognized Ali's devotion to his faith and ruled that he had been treated unfairly. American citizens have the right to refuse military service because of their religion. Ali did not have to pay a fine or go to jail.

Ali was nearly twenty-nine years old when he returned to boxing. He had lost some of his speed. Some people believed his days as a winner in the boxing ring were over. Ali proved them wrong, winning his first fight against Jerry Quarry by a knockout in the third round. By the time he went up against Argentine boxer Oscar Bonavena, he was writing poems again.

His poem about the Bonavena fight ended with:

Before Round Nine is out
The referee will jump and shout
"THAT'S ALL, FOLKS
this turkey is out!"

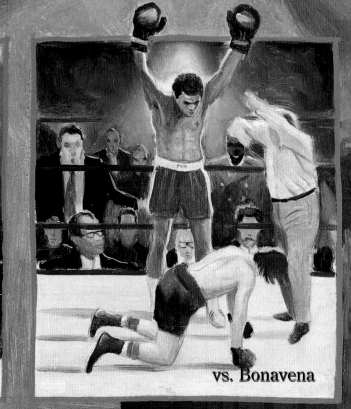

vs. Quarry

vs. Bonavena

vs. Frazier, 1971

This time, his prediction did not come true. It took him fifteen rounds to knock out Bonavena. On March 8, 1971, Ali went up against the world heavyweight champion Joe Frazier. Ali was almost knocked out, and the judges awarded the win to Frazier. It was the first loss of his professional career. Ali accepted the defeat, but he declared that he wanted to fight Frazier again.

Three years passed, and many of Ali's matches lasted much longer than they had when he was younger. He had his jaw broken in a fight against Ken Norton for his second loss.

Meanwhile, Joe Frazier lost the heavyweight title to George Foreman. Finally, the two ex-champions, Ali and Frazier, had their rematch. This time Ali outboxed Frazier. The judges awarded him the win. Now, Ali could go up against Foreman for the heavyweight boxing crown.

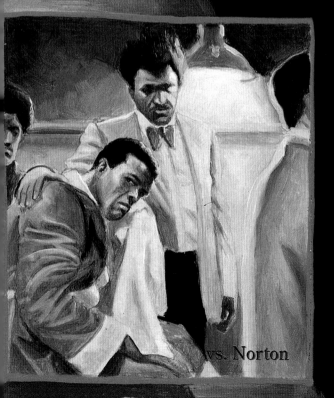

vs. Norton

vs. Frazier, 1974

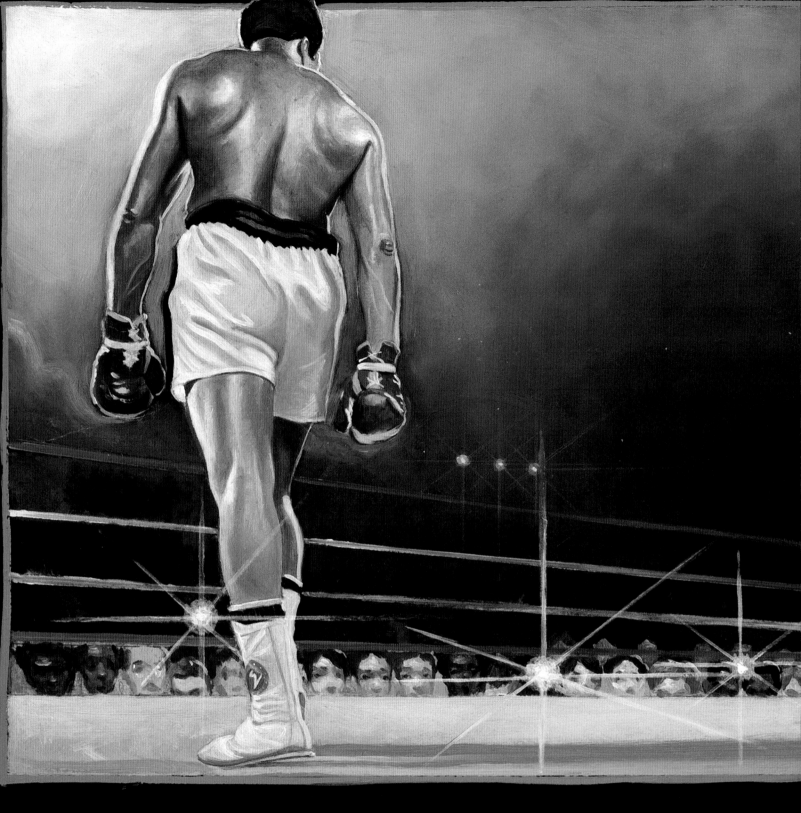

By 1974, Foreman had won all twenty-four of his professional fights by knockouts. Ali trained harder than he ever had before. The fight was staged in the African nation of Zaire and was billed as the "Rumble in the Jungle." It was a proud moment for all of black Africa, which was fighting against white South Africa's support of racism. Ali hoped it would be a proud moment for him. He knew it was going to be a tough fight. Foreman was younger and stronger. Nevertheless, Ali was faster and more experienced. He knocked down Foreman in the eighth round, and the referee counted him out. After seven long years, Muhammad Ali had won his title back.

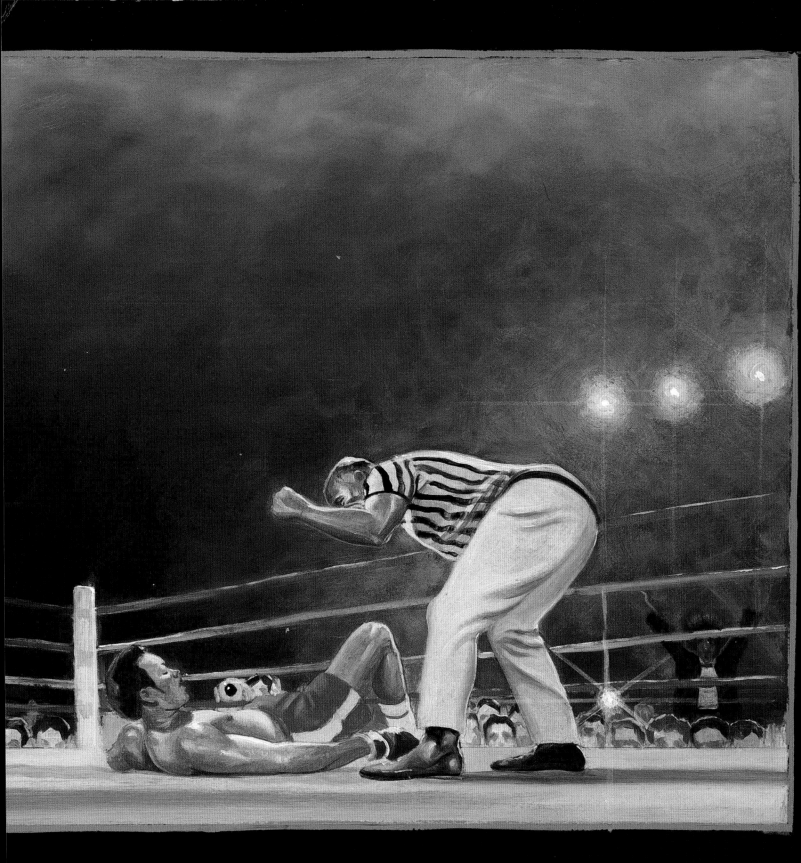

During those years, Ali had also won respect. Most Americans had come to believe that the United States was wrong to fight in Vietnam. They admired Ali for standing up to the government. They also understood that he was sincere in his religious faith. He had not tried to escape from the draft by using religion as an excuse. He remained a devoted follower of world Islam.

Ali said many times that he would know when it was time to retire. He wanted to leave boxing before he was seriously injured. He believed that his style of boxing protected him. As he put it in one of his poems:

In the ring I can stay
Until I'm old and gray
Because I know how to hit
And dance away

His style depended on speed, however, and he was slowing down. He had to learn how to take a punch. Although he won many bouts, he was injured several times. His third and

final bout in 1975 against Joe Frazier in the Philippines, known as "The Thrilla in Manila," is considered by many to be the greatest boxing match of all time. Ali won, but at great cost. He took nearly 440 punches during that one fight.

In 1978, after defending his title successfully ten times, he lost it to Leon Spinks. He regained the title by beating Spinks seven months later and became the first boxer to win the heavyweight championship three times. He then announced his retirement.

Sadly, against the wishes of his friends and family, he returned to the ring for two more bouts in 1980 and 1981 and lost both. At thirty-nine years old, he was beginning to suffer from brain damage. He looked the same, but he sometimes had trouble speaking. His reflexes were slowing and his movements could be stiff. Boxing had given him an incurable condition called Parkinson's Syndrome. It does not threaten his life, or affect his intelligence, but it does steadily erode his control over his own body.

Since retiring from the boxing ring, Muhammad Ali has enjoyed his life. Although he doesn't live there now, his heart has always stayed in his hometown of Louisville, Kentucky, where his brother, Rudy, still lives. Ali intends to build a Muhammad Ali center to train young boys in the sport that gave him so much.

Ali is close to his fourth wife, Lonnie, and to his nine children. He was not around much when the older children were growing up, so he especially enjoys playing with the youngest, Asaad, whom he and Lonnie adopted. Asaad, and the many people who visit, enjoy the magic tricks that Ali does to entertain them. Ali remains a devout Muslim and prays five times a day. He considers himself the world's goodwill ambassador and appears in public quite often, although he rarely speaks.

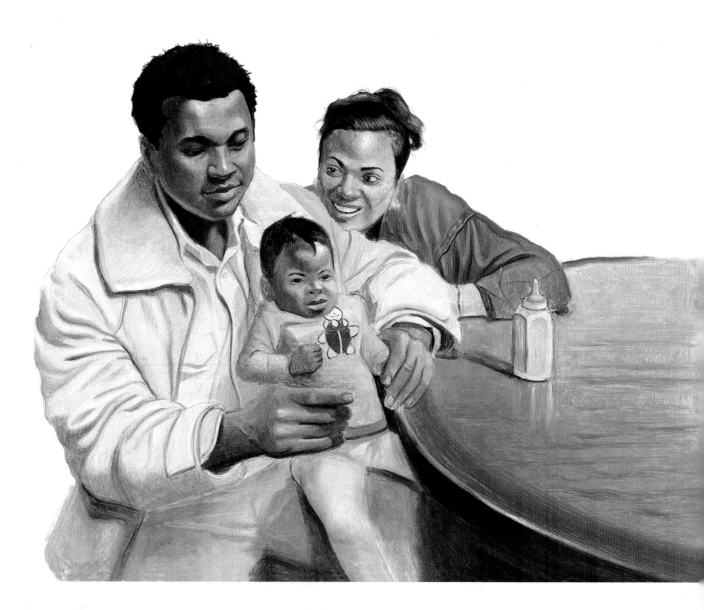

In 1996, Muhammad Ali made a surprise appearance at the Summer Olympics in Atlanta, Georgia. He was the final bearer of the torch that lights the Olympic flame and opens the games. His arm shook as he held the symbol of international sporting competition. No one had expected him, and the crowd in the stadium and the billions of television watchers throughout the world cheered with love and respect. Ali was as much a symbol himself as was the torch. He was a symbol of strength and skill, of courage and pride. He was a man who broke down barriers and who brought people together—a champion in more ways than one.

CHRONOLOGY

1942   Born in Louisville, Kentucky, January 17

1959   Wins Golden Gloves Championship in Chicago

1960   Wins Olympic gold medal in Rome; turns professional

1964   Beats Sonny Liston to become heavyweight champion of the world;
announces his membership in the Nation of Islam

1965   Beats Liston in a rematch; defends his title against Floyd Patterson

1966   Wins five more fights, four by knockouts

1967   Wins two more fights, one by knockout; refuses to be inducted into the army and is sentenced
to five years in jail; his lawyers appeal the sentence; has his boxing license suspended

1967-70   Gives speeches against the Vietnam War at colleges during his ban from boxing

1970   Regains his license and wins his first two fights

1971   Loses to heavyweight champion Joe Frazier; five-year jail sentence reversed;
wins three later fights

1972   Wins six fights, four by knockouts

1973   Fights four times; has his jaw broken by Ken Norton, but wins the rematch

1974   Beats Joe Frazier; knocks out George Foreman to reclaim the heavyweight boxing crown

1975-78   After successfully defending his title ten times, loses heavyweight crown to Leon Spinks;
beats Leon Spinks in rematch to regain heavyweight crown, the first boxer to win the crown
three times

1979   Announces his retirement from boxing

1980-81   Comes out of retirement; loses his last two bouts against Larry Holmes and Trevor Berbick

1996   Lights the torch to open the Olympic Games in Atlanta, Georgia

SELECTED BIBLIOGRAPHY

For adults

Ali, Muhammad, with Richard Durham. *The Greatest: My Own Story.* New York: Random House, 1975

Hauser, Thomas. *Muhammad Ali: His Life and Times.* New York: Simon & Schuster, 1991

Remnick, David. *King of the World: Muhammad Ali and the Rise of an American Hero.* New York: Random House, 1998

For middle grade and teen readers

Conklin, Thomas. *Muhammad Ali: The Fight for Respect.* Brookfield, CT: Millbrook, 1994

Denenberg, Barry. *The Story of Muhammad Ali: Heavyweight Champion of the World.* New York: Dell, 1990

Freedman, Suzanne. *Clay V. United States: Muhammad Ali Objects to War.* Springfield, NJ: Enslow, 1997

Garrett, Leslie. *The Story of Muhammad Ali.* New York: Dorling Kindersley, 2002

Gordon, Randy. *Muhammad Ali.* New York: Penguin Putnam, 2001

Hook, Jason. *Muhammad Ali: The Greatest.* Austin, TX: Raintree/Steck Vaughn, 2001

Lewis, Jon E. *The Life and Times of Muhammad Ali.* New York: Chelsea House, 1997

Macht, Norman. *Muhammad Ali: the People's Champion.* New York: Chelsea House, 1994

Myers, Walter Dean. *The Greatest: Muhammad Ali.* New York: Scholastic, 2001

Rummel, Jack. *Muhammad Ali: Heavyweight Champion.* New York: Chelsea House, 1988

Schulman, Arlene. *Muhammad Ali.* Minneapolis, MN: Lerner, 2000

Tessitore, John. *Muhammad Ali: The World's Champion.* New York: Franklin Watts, 1998

SEE FIST

OR THE HEAVYWEIG

BO

TO

THE MAIN

SEE THE GR